AF382656

12 RULES FOR LIFE: AN ANTIDOTE TO CHAOS

A guide to meaning in the modern world

Summary & Analysis of
Jordan Peterson's book

12 RULES FOR LIFE: AN ANTIDOTE TO CHAOS

A GUIDE TO CONSCIOUS NAVIGATION OF THE KNOWN (ORDER) SO YOUR LIFE CAN BENEFIT FROM THE POSITIVE UNKNOWN (CREATIVITY AND EXPLORATION) AND ENDURE THE ONSLAUGHT OF CHAOS THAT WOULD UNNECESSARILY INCREASE SUFFERING IN THIS WORLD

12 Rules for Life seeks to draw on millennia of gathered wisdom conveyed through the drama of mythology and the unavoidable instincts of eons of evolution to promote the minimisation of unnecessary suffering in life. In an academic landscape dominated by post-modernism and niche Marxism, Peterson seeks to rearticulate wisdom for life that appreciates, rather than rejects, the insight humanity encoded in its myths. Taoism symbolises the balance of order and chaos in the yin and yang symbol, each side showing the emergence of its opposite within itself. Consciousness navigates and mediates these opposing forces for an optimal life.

Key information

- **Reference edition:** Peterson, J. B. (2018) *12 Rules for Life.* London: Penguin Random House.
- **1st edition:** 2018
- **Author:** Jordan B. Peterson (clinical psychologist and professor of psychology, b. 1962)
- **Fields:** self-help, psychology
- **Key words:**
  - Order: the realm of the known, familiar, and dependable. Order is the predictable and established track on which the train of life progresses. An excess of order oppressively excludes what is "other" for the sake of uniform identity. It is allegorically considered a masculine entity.
  - Chaos: an experience of ignorance. It is anything new and unexplored. As unrestrained liberty, it can either

quicken creativity or instead crush your soul as it redefines your expectations in life. It is allegorically considered a feminine entity.

- ◦ <u>Being</u>: the entirety of subjective human experience.

CONTEXT

THE AUTHOR

Raised in Northern Alberta, the University of Toronto professor of psychology Jordan Peterson is a clinical psychologist. He spent part of his career lecturing at Harvard. With associates and pupils, he has published over a hundred papers. He has a significant online presence, with YouTube hosting scores of hours of his lectures, multiple debates and interviews. Peterson is also present on Twitter and Instagram, collecting hundreds of thousands of followers. Beyond universities and clinics, his insight has been sought by corporate and political bodies, including a report to the UN Secretary General on global sustainability. He and his wife Tammy have raised two children: Mikhaila and Julian.

CONTEXT AND BACKGROUND

One of the primary influences on Jordan Peterson was Carl Jung (Swiss psychiatrist and psychoanalyst, 1875-1961). Jung's approach to psychoanalysis, particularly focused on ancient mythology, directs much of Peterson's approach. Alexandr Solzhenitsyn's (Russian writer and dissident, 1918-2008) *Gulag Archipelago* (1973) informs much of what Peterson seeks to correct for individuals who read this book. The Marxist philosophy, whose adherents have been responsible for tens of millions of deaths in the last 100 years, has pervaded much of Western thought in the quest for equality and resistance to any form of hierarchy. Materialistic evolution and post-modernism dispense with much wisdom, from Peterson's perspective, by rejecting mythology in its entirety:

> "In the West, we have been withdrawing from our tradition-, religion- and even nation-centred cultures, partly to decrease the danger of group conflict. But we are increasingly falling prey to the desperation of meaninglessness, and that is no improvement at all" (p. xxxii)

Peterson looks to minimise unnecessary suffering by providing the individual with the wisdom necessary to live a meaningful life.

SUMMARY OF 12 RULES FOR LIFE

RULE 1: "STAND UP STRAIGHT WITH YOUR SHOULDERS BACK." (P. 1)

Your position in the hierarchy you find yourself in has a biological effect on you. Lobsters are relatively uncomplicated to study neurologically but provide a valuable insight into the ancestral template from which humans and lobsters both developed. Lobsters claim territory and defend it against interlopers. The stronger the lobster, the more capable he is of claiming nutrient-rich, prime real estate and defending it. Approaches by other males initiate challenges, which will result in a winner and a loser even if one avoids conflict by retreat. The lobster's status ranks his standing among his neighbourhood of lobsters. The outcome of a conflict changes the balance of chemicals in the lobster brain (the ratio favours serotonin on winning and octopamine on losing). A winning lobster feels more confident and has higher standing because of his victory. A losing lobster becomes disproportionately more likely to lose in future confrontations, even though his strength and skill may have been enough to previously carry him to victory. The loser adopts a lower posture and thus reinforces his downward spiral. He loses additional territory, food, and mating opportunities by his submissive posture. Supposing a third lobster does not seize on the victor's vulnerability after battle, the victor becomes desirable to females looking to mate. A hierarchy like this is not a human construct but a fact of evolution that precedes the emergence of any sort of ape. Despite philosophies that attribute hierarchy to the bourgeoisie or patriarchy, Nature is its source. Nature, simultaneously characterised as inert and vibrant, chooses the adaptable to survive. Higher status increases one's chances of being adaptable and thus surviving. The chemical balance in lobsters is reflected in humans and produces similar results. People with high levels of serotonin (winners) generally demonstrate better health, live longer lives, and gather more resources in every social stratum. Those with low levels of serotonin (non-winners) are more likely to suffer ill health and die sooner. While there are definitely outside factors that contribute to these results, the two chemicals that respond to victories and defeats prime your biological state. This biological state, either confidence or alertness, set you on a path, through habitual repetition, into a "feedback loop." Winning produces confidence, which prepares you to win again. Losing sets you on edge and puts you in a defensive posture, which increases your chances of losing at the next challenge. But you can jump start an upward spiral by adopting an upright posture, as opposed to slouching and drooping, so your body feels like a winner. This new attitude must be accompanied by action that validates it, however small, so as to encourage the development of positive chemical reinforcement. Push towards purposes of truth and meaning against the forces, personal or ethereal, that subdue you. Every small step will increase your momentum towards your goal. Incorporating this approach into your life can help set you on a fresh footing to make the most of the opportunities that face you.

RULE 2: "TREAT YOURSELF LIKE SOMEONE YOU ARE RESPONSIBLE FOR HELPING." (P. 31)

Statistics for patient medication usage suggest something odd about people. One third of patients do not even fill their prescription. One third fill the prescription but are not committed to finishing the course, or skip individual doses. That leaves one in three people prescribed a medication who take it as instructed. Contrast this with the people who will take their sick pet to the vet and then ensure that the animal gets every dose of its medication regularly, in spite of the animal's objections. Apparently, people care less about their own welfare than they care about the welfare of those in their charge.

Ancient wisdom helps us navigate life, particularly in regard to suffering. A stable life will find a way to incorporate the structure offered by order and the opportunity and exploration offered by chaos, without descending into the extreme of either (order leading to harsh domination and chaos leading to volatile and frightening uncertainty). The Genesis account of Adam and Eve describes the result of cognisance of self as disgrace and self-loathing, especially in the presence of "the Ideal" (p. 50). The suffering of Being is a result of self-awareness, as God pronounced the curse on Adam and Eve for taking the knowledge of good and evil. And so, why don't we take care of ourselves? Perhaps we hold ourselves in disdain because we are fully aware of our own failings. Denying ourselves help may be a self-appointed penance for our guilt. Beyond our failings, inside each of us there are strands of evil — humans cause suffering purely to see others suffer. Rather than destroying ourselves for our transgressions, we must recognise our value and importance in this world and maximise that latent potential. Making a difference to others, and respecting yourself, by minimising suffering and telling the truth will allow you to expiate the failings for which you punish yourself. A first step might be to nurture and support yourself like you would another person.

RULE 3: "MAKE FRIENDS WITH PEOPLE WHO WANT THE BEST FOR YOU." (P. 67)

Sometimes people in a bad place will choose friends who will reinforce that state. As the saying goes, misery loves company. Hopeless and aimless friends are not looking to encourage growth and progress in their peers. Unfortunately, befriending people who are intent on destroying their lives rarely helps them and likely harms you. Desperation or determination to change presents the moment to best help that person. Until they want to grow, there is little you can do to help. Your growth and intention to develop passes judgment on those who refuse to grow. Do not let your friends hold you back. Choose friends who themselves are improving and want that for you too.

RULE 4: "COMPARE YOURSELF WITH WHO YOU WERE YESTERDAY, NOT TO WHO SOMEONE ELSE IS TODAY." (P. 85)

Our lives are overly connected with those of other people. The natural tendency towards personal comparison, which may have proved helpful in providing goals for growth living in a small community, has become overwhelming in the age of social media. Life can be described as multiple, simultaneous games. No one else faces the exact combination of challenges that you face with the precise level of opportunity and resources. You are responsible for making the most of your life, not for wining at someone else's game. Bargain with yourself to maximise your own output and your victories, and keep your word to yourself about rewards. You need to enlist your own cooperation to win. Let your unique desires and responsibilities form your conditions for victory. Stand up for yourself, not allowing these desires and responsibilities to be crushed by the tyranny of others. "We only see what we aim at," (p. 101); in other words, you cannot discern a path different from the direction you have set. Your target should be your own improvement and the improvement of the lives of those around you. Ultimately you "decide to act as if existence might be justified by its goodness—if only you behaved properly," (p. 107). This path may start with the smallest step you **can** and **will** take towards improvement. You can only discern those steps by listening to yourself and being aware of your own willingness to cooperate with your new changes. Pursue the greatest impact for good in life while also taking care of the moment's tasks. You must realise that making progress in the unique combination of challenges in your own life cannot be measured against the life of someone playing different games.

RULE 5: "DO NOT LET YOUR CHILDREN DO ANYTHING THAT MAKES YOU DISLIKE THEM." (P. 113)

Parents who avoid the unpleasant momentary confrontation of correcting their children end up constantly supervising them to protect them, rather than simply teaching the child the boundaries of safety and propriety. Children are not Rousseau's (Genevan philosopher, 1712-1778) "blank slate" who require only the absence of corrupting influence to turn out well. Children contain enough good and evil to destroy or build up. They are pleasant and innocent and selfish and destructive. Civilisation restrains personal violence, not absolutely but demonstrably. Parents bear the responsibility of equipping their child to restrain their own worse impulses and develop their better ones so they will be welcomed by society. Society will reject and punish those adults who did not learn as children how to contribute rather than leech in their relationships. Although it might seem counterintuitive, structure enables the free flow of creativity. Consistent encouragement of good behaviour and confrontation of bad behaviour allows the child to prioritise and subjugate their own desires. The best life for a child is offered by loving structure that prepares it to one day take its place in society, as an integrated, independent contributor not as a mindless drone. A few regulations, the fewer and simpler the better, should be imposed by means of the minimum required constraint. You must help your child without becoming an overbearing tyrant or bully. Help them be kind to other children, polite to adults, and go to sleep at bedtime. This will help them become desirable company, friends, employees, and partners. This venture will likely include some physical correction, but, again, you only should employ the minimum force required to constrain your child's wrong behaviour. A mild flick can correct a toddler. Timeout corners can help angry children. Particularly innovative and persistent monstrous behaviour may require a traditional spanking, but that is not the first recourse. Parents should be committed to correcting their children's behaviour, because the world is not a forgiving place for impulsive and selfish adults.

RULE 6: "SET YOUR HOUSE IN PERFECT ORDER BEFORE YOU CRITICIZE THE WORLD." (P. 147)

Being inevitably involves suffering. Some people conclude that this suffering cannot not be justified and the only recourse is vengeance on humanity, often culminating in murder-suicide. The Columbine shooters recorded their hatred and desire for retribution to those who had made them suffer. They embarked on their course of retaliation before ending their own existence and suffering. The story of Cain and Abel demonstrates this tendency of the suffering to punish the virtuous in response to unfair circumstances. God refused Cain's sacrifice so Cain murdered his brother, who had pleased God. Some conclude, as Tolstoy (Russian novelist, 1828-1910) did, that death is the only reasonable escape from the suffering of Being. But perhaps we can minimise suffering by taking responsibility for our mistakes and transgressions. By taking ownership and restraining those choices that would increase our suffering, good can unfold. Good makes suffering bearable. A life where consciousness balances order and chaos will seek what is best and minimise the suffering amplified by unrestrained chaos.

Without additional suffering, a soul fortified by goodness can put up with most of the suffering inherent to fragile creatures. Rather than passing judgment on others, take responsibility for your own life. Cease activities that shame and weaken you. Instead, do what is right and best.

RULE 7: "PURSUE WHAT IS MEANINGFUL (NOT WHAT IS EXPEDIENT.)" (P. 161)

When humanity travelled as bands of hunters or learned to farm, appreciation grew for the idea of keeping surplus to use later. Rather than eating all the crop, some was kept for planting. The more that was sacrificed in the present, the better the future could be. The more you had in the future, the more you could provide for others and thus build your status in the community: "The successful among us delay gratification. The successful among us bargain with the future," (p. 169). Through the Genesis narrative, we see how our ancestors felt the importance of sacrifice to please God was an aspect of wisdom for all. The pursuit of meaning and goodness in this life will require sacrifice. Valuing future pleasures above current ones, be they innocent or evil, promotes a life that will reject shortcuts to achieve gain. Convenience and shortcuts easily lead to evil actions. Evil is inflicting suffering on others needlessly. A life governed by convenience is short-sighted, willing to sacrifice what is best in the future for an immediate advantage. This undermines your ability to best help yourself and others later. Since we at least recognise that we want to live a life that is not evil, we are then led to the realisation that we should want to live a life that is good.

> "If there is something that is not good, then there is something that is good. If the worst sin is the torment of others, merely for the sake of the suffering produced — then the good is whatever is diametrically opposed to that. The good is whatever stops such things from happening." (p. 198)

If that is good, then a life of virtue, of meaning, will curtail needless suffering. Meaning guides the consciousness to navigate chaos and order, providing the most responsible use of creativity and structure to alleviate suffering. Expedience short-circuits that intention. A life of meaning requires sacrifice in the present to guarantee a better future.

RULE 8: "TELL THE TRUTH — OR, AT LEAST, DON'T LIE." (P. 203)

Someone who tells the truth is not trying to hijack reality. Such a person is humbled before the vast flow of reality and know the best course is found by surrounding themselves with as much accuracy as possible. If you feel that you know all you need to forecast the best outcome in your life and believe that unfolding events must be controlled for the best results, then you are likely in danger of manipulating by your words and distancing yourself from the truth. The truth provides the most consistent and helpful direction in life. The truth will help you correct your behaviour when you miss your target, whereas falsehoods will shift the responsibility, and with it your hope of remedy, to others. "If you betray yourself, if you say untrue things, if you act out a lie, you weaken your character" (p. 212), and trouble will overwhelm you in such an anaemic state. To be consistent in the face of trouble, suffering, and evil, you must consistently tell the truth. Your silence or manipulations will only inflame situations in the long term. Lying betrays an arrogance against reality that corrupts a Being. Speaking the truth strengthens your soul to endure life's problems and offers firmer footing as you move forward.

RULE 9: "ASSUME THAT THE PERSON YOU ARE LISTENING TO MIGHT KNOW SOMETHING YOU DON'T." (P. 233)

We need better information and conclusions to improve our lives. To achieve that, we need the challenge offered by a dissenting voice. Some can appropriate this benefit by thinking deeply about their situation: "Thinking is an internal dialogue between two or more different views of the world," (p. 241). This interaction allows you to modify your thoughts and intentions to be more accurate, integrating more possibilities into your process. This discipline is hard, so often people talk to others rather than themselves. To benefit in the same way, however, the other party must spend most of their time listening, not speaking. A person engaged in listening will offer non-verbal cues that allow the speaker unconsciously to modify their intentions or perspective. "People organize their brains with conversation" (p. 250).

We must provide that opportunity in support of others. Often, people view discussions as opportunities for supremacy by fighting — often fighting dirty — for their previously held positions. A true listener, in contrast, engages with the speaker and helps them formulate the best conclusions of their line of thought. A sophisticated situation can develop where participants in a conversation adopt the role of both speaker and listener, mutually furthering a thought to its best conclusion without concern for an apparent social victory. This approach to life rests on the understanding that you do not know everything, not even everything that you need to know, and that other people can help you discover that helpful knowledge.

RULE 10: "BE PRECISE IN YOUR SPEECH." (P. 259)

Ambiguous goals and responses to problems promote chaos. Humanity has the ability to focus on very few of the infinite interactions in our world. This is true for optical vision as well as our perception and intentions. Crises seem sudden and overwhelming because our perception is overcome when situations force themselves into our narrow focus. Precision becomes a key tool in either avoiding or managing these problems. The accurate statement of goals defines the conditions for victory or defeat. The accurate definition of a crisis isolates it and prepares you to find a solution. It might feel like the world has fallen apart, but really it only one limited set of circumstances. Do not avoid hard issues or topics of discussion. Overlooked failings or sins fester and grow until they require radical intervention. Many times, divorce is the conclusion of a marriage that ignored small issues until the cumulative result was a chasm separating two people who used to be in love. Your precision in speech will allow you and those close to you to know who you really are. It will help mitigate the onslaught of chaos as you progress through life.

RULE 11: "DO NOT BOTHER CHILDREN WHEN THEY ARE SKATEBOARDING." (P. 285)

Several philosophies in the last century have conspired to suppress individual competence and excellence. Marxist foundations see left-leaning thinkers inclined to pursue an equity of outcome that curtails free development of the individual. Political communism has murdered tens of millions who were more prosperous than their countrymen, or whose individual thought and expression threatened the establishment. Despite these atrocities, philosophers have defended Marxist doctrine and sought innovative ways to apply it throughout society as if the violence were anomalous and not a direct result of its underlying suppositions. The primary tool of Western Marxist and post-modern thought is the education system — kindergarten through university — where the next generation of teachers are trained to claim more ground as the cycle begins again. Any form of hierarchy poses a threat to the goal of equality. The patriarchy poses a particular threat as it has supposedly subjugated women for millennia. Boys must be indoctrinated against any form of assertive behaviour that would perpetuate the cycle. But the underlying assumption is unproven and false. Until quite recently, men and women cooperated, taking on different roles, simply to survive an impoverished existence. As technology has developed, particularly mass-produced feminine hygiene products and birth control but also advances that make rewarding labour less reliant on upper-body strength, there are more choices in the cooperation between men and women. When starvation stops being a pressing concern, people are freer to make meaningful, personal choices in vocation. When choosing an occupation, it can be generally stated that "Boys' interests tilt towards things; girls' interests tilt towards people" (p. 298). Forcing women into STEM fields and men into elementary education or nursing in the name of equity undermines the freedom and value of the individual. While the movement for women's equal opportunities may not have finished its work, it has finished the lion's share. The remainder should not, however, seek to undermine anyone's pursuit of competence and excellence. Let young boys try to get better at skateboarding, even though it is dangerous. Let them grow without an absolute dependence on their mother (or more broadly any authority) to make life safe and comfortable. Allow boys grow into determined and capable men who pursue good in themselves and others.

RULE 12: "PET A CAT WHEN YOU ENCOUNTER ONE ON THE STREET." (P. 335)

The reality of suffering invades our lives to various degrees daily. In response to this intrusion, you can cower or ignore it, but it is more meaningful to endure it and minimise the suffering of others. More than enduring, life sends little moments of joy and light to remind you that goodness justifies Being.

> "And maybe when you are going for a walk and your head is spinning a cat will show up and if you pay attention to it then you will get a reminder for just fifteen seconds that the wonder of Being might make up for the ineradicable suffering that accompanies it." (p. 353)

As you have aimed high — you seek to improve life and minimise suffering — and are taking responsibility and telling the truth, enjoy the little moments that underline the miracle of existence.

IMPACT OF 12 RULES FOR LIFE

RECEPTION

According to Peterson's website, this book has sold millions of copies and was "#1 for nonfiction in 2018 in the US, Canada, the UK, Australia, New Zealand, Sweden, the Netherlands, Brazil and Norway, and now slated for translation into 45 languages." The publisher can clip several recommendations from well-known publications such as *The Times*, *The Guardian*, and the *Toronto Star*. The *Toronto Star* comments,

> "Like the best intellectual polymaths, Peterson invites his readers to embark on their own intellectual, spiritual and ideological journeys into the many topics and disciplines he touches on. It's a counter-intuitive strategy for a population hooked on the instant gratification of ideological conformity and social media 'likes,' but if Peterson is right, you have nothing to lose but your own misery." (Grainger, 2018)

And Melanie Reid of *The Times* adds,

> "Grow up and man up is the message from this rock-star psychologist… [A] hardline self-help manual of self-reliance, good behaviour, self-betterment and individualism that probably reflects his childhood in rural Canada in the 1960s. As with all self-help manuals, there's always a kernel of truth. Formerly a Harvard professor, now at the University of Toronto, Peterson retains that whiff of cowboy philosophy—one essay is a homily on doing one thing every day to improve yourself. Another, on bringing up little children to behave, is excellent…. [Peterson] twirls ideas around like a magician." (2018)

Peterson is an accomplished clinical psychologist and professor of psychology. Opposition to his book tends to be more based on his philosophy than his credentials. Peterson attempts to summarise ancient wisdom for a contemporary audience. Although he personally considers himself more of a liberal, this conservative wisdom contradicts several new social norms regarding the uniformity of socialism, gender roles, and child-rearing and thus earns criticism from some journalists and bloggers. In spite of this division, Peterson's promotional lectures have taken him through North America, Europe, and Australia to speak to over 200 000 people interested in this message.

CRITICISMS OF PETERSON'S APPROACH

12 Rules for Life reflects the author's ability as a professor to present a topic for consideration, much like a university lecture. He introduces the topic, connects it with real life by sharing past experiences, presents some of the research that explains why we should change our thinking and behaviour, discusses that, then brings it to the resolution by a statement which also serves as the chapter heading. It could be argued that Peterson should offer more discussion and support for his conclusions; however, Peterson previously published a weighty work called *Maps of Meaning*, which contains much deeper thought and academic investigation, and is not as accessible as *12 Rules for Life*. Peterson offers enough discussion and support for people looking to him for help, but not enough to dissuade people who take the opposite viewpoint. *12 Rules for Life* forces some serious personal thought and reflection, assuming a predisposition towards accepting this advice.

Some of the reliance on mythological descriptions of order and chaos as masculine and feminine create ambiguity regarding Peterson's advice for men and women. Peterson starts with the historic viewpoints of these forces and advocates consciousness navigating life with these two in balance. The book's subtitle, *An Antidote to Chaos*, seems to suggest the need for masculinity to correct the imbalance created by femininity. Peterson does not seem to be arguing from a misogynistic motivation. Discussing chaos and order is not about men versus women, but people finding balance in the face of entities characterised by gender. Peterson stated in an interview that the book might serve as an antidote to order if our society were under the tyranny of excessive order rather than in the throes of chaotic disintegration. Peterson argues for balance of these forces. Too much order results in totalitarian oppression, even on an individual level. Too much chaos leads to oppression by the unknown and the fear that accompanies it. Even when, in Rule 11, he seeks to argue that young boys should not be converted to the temperamental characteristics of young girls, as if masculine traits were undesirable, Peterson does not argue that young girls must learn masculine traits to bring "order". The assignment of genders to order and chaos is a matter of history, but it leads to some confusion when a book which offers advice to a society redefining rights and responsibilities in light of gender bases its foundational premise on categories discussed as gendered personalities. *12 Rules for Life* seeks to equip people to live meaningful lives by navigating chaos and order in balance. It is not suggesting that men need to oppress women to find value.

SUMMARY

- Peterson's aim in this book is to help people find meaning in their lives by taking responsibility and telling the truth. Being does involve suffering, but some suffering can be limited. Unrestrained chaos amplifies suffering, but a life moderated by order can limit suffering. With integrity and character, the suffering introduced by the march of Nature or the evil of others can be endured. Then the joys of life offer validation for the choice to pursue what is meaningful.

- Peterson believes that unnecessary suffering can be minimised if we follow good advice. Good advice was preserved in myths because it made life work. Western culture has hurt itself by rejecting that wisdom just because myths are not scientific fact. Peterson provides studies from Genesis and the Gospels, Eastern mythology, and European fairy tales to help us life a life of meaning. He believes that these stories dramatically encoded directions for life that surpass the cold observation of the material world.

- This book offers hope that when someone embraces personal responsibility, that person can minimise unnecessary suffering in their life and the lives of others.
- Anecdotally, in multiple interviews, Peterson reports hundreds of responses of gratitude, either in person or by correspondence, for his direction in changing lives (ranging from restored familial relationships to prevention of suicide).

We want to hear from you!
Leave a comment on your online library
and share your favourite books on social media!

FURTHER READING

BIBLIOGRAPHY

- (No date) About Jordan Peterson. *Jordanbpeterson. com*. [Online]. [Accessed 22 January 2019]. Available from: <https://jordanbpeterson.com/about/>

- (2018) Channel 4 News Interview. *Youtube. com*. [Online]. [Accessed 29 January 2019]. Available from: <https://www.youtube.com/watch?v=aMcjxSThD54>

- (2018) Fox News Interview. *Youtube.com*. [Online]. [Accessed 29 January 2019]. Available from: https://www.youtube.com/watch?v=XTg_NJy-Eis

- Grainger, J. (2018) Jordan Peterson on embracing your inner lobster in 12 Rules for Life. *Toronto Star*. [Online]. [Accessed 29 January 2019]. Available from: <https://www.thestar.com/entertainment/books/2018/01/22/jordan-peterson-on-embracing-your-inner-lobster-in-12-rules-for-life.html>

- (2018) Martin Weill Interview. *Youtube. com*. [Online]. [Accessed 29 January 2019]. Available from: <https://www.youtube.com/watch?v=CzZDed4gEHc>

- Peterson, J. B. (2018) *12 Rules for Life*. London: Penguin Random House.

- (2018) Real Time with Bill Maher Interview. *Youtube.com.* [Online]. [Accessed 29 January 2019]. Available from: <https://www.youtube.com/watch?v=8wLCmDtCDAM>

- Reid, M. (2018) Review: 12 Rules for Life: An Antidote to Chaos. *The Times.* [Online]. [Accessed 29 January 2019]. Available from: <https://www.thetimes.co.uk/article/review-12-rules-for-life-anantidote-to-chaos-by-jordan-b-peterson-hv3dx0rwz>

- (2017) The Rubin Report Interview. *Youtube.com.* [Online]. [Accessed 29 January 2019]. Available from: <https://www.youtube.com/watch?v=GJJClhqGq_M>

- (2018) Vice News Interview. *Youtube.com.* [Online]. [Accessed 29 January 2019]. Available from: <https://www.youtube.com/watch?v=blTglME9rvQ>

ADDITIONAL SOURCES

- Peterson's official website: https://jordanbpeterson.com/

- Jung, C. (1991) *Aion: Researches into the Phenomenology of the Self.* London: Routledge.

- Peterson, J. B. (1999) *Maps of Meaning: The Architecture of Belief.* New York: Routledge.

- Solzhenitsyn, A. (2018) *Gulag Archipelago with a foreword by Jordan B. Peterson.* London: Vintage.

50MINUTES.com
History
Business
Coaching
Book Review
Health & Wellbeing
IMPROVE YOUR
GENERAL KNOWLEDGE
IN A BLINK OF AN EYE !
www.50minutes.com

Although the editor makes every effort to verify the accuracy of the information published, 50Minutes.com accepts no responsibility for the content of this book.

© 50MINUTES.com, 2019. All rights reserved.

www.50minutes.com

Ebook EAN: 9782808017244

Paperback EAN: 9782808017251

Legal Deposit: D/2019/12603/29

Cover: © Primento

Digital conception by Primento, the digital partner of publishers.